PAST & PRESENT

POCATELLO

While on tour in 1902, Pres. Theodore Roosevelt stopped in Pocatello to give a speech at Pocatello High School. Since the school was the only one in town, it was a major meeting spot for any large gathering. This banner over Center Street featured a picture of President Roosevelt. This was the first time a president had stopped in Pocatello, and the town wanted to make a big celebration of it.

Past & Present

POCATELLO

Joshua Kiggins

For my Nana and Papa, who collected so many postcards over the years and helped me become more interested in the history of my hometown, Pocatello. Had I not inherited this collection, who knows how I would've harnessed this energy.

ISBN 978-1-4671-0658-0

Library of Congress Control Number: 2021930142

Published by Arcadia Publishing
Charleston, South Carolina

Printed in the United States of America

For all general information, please contact Arcadia Publishing:
Telephone 843-853-2070
Fax 843-853-0044
E-mail sales@arcadiapublishing.com
For customer service and orders:
Toll-Free 1-888-313-2665

Visit us on the Internet at www.arcadiapublishing.com

On the Front Cover: In 1907, Pocatello was rapidly growing and expanding. As part of this growth, knowledge was becoming more important, and so, like many cities around the world, Pocatello received a Carnegie Library. Here it is in 1909, a couple years after completion. The house to the left was donated for the librarian to live in. An addition and atrium were built in 1993 to expand usable space. Currently, the original building is used as offices for library staff. (All images from the author's collection.)

On the Back Cover: This Railroad Young Men's Christian Association, built in 1907, was the third in Pocatello due to an increase in population. Two additions were built in the 1910s, when it served as barracks for soldiers traveling between here and Fort Lewis, Washington. A fire destroyed the building in 1963, and the rebuilt portion that opened in 1965 was only a third the size. The YMCA moved to a fourth location in 1979, and the building was razed in 1986. (Author's collection.).

Contents

Acknowledgments

To my family, thank you for instilling the love for history and for always being there to help push me along to do my best.

To my friends, thank you for letting me be me and share my love of history and even feigning interest, though you might have been bored.

To the people of Pocatello, the experiences I had and the people I grew up with, positive and negative, helped me get to where I am today and attain this amazing achievement. The people are what make communities great.

To Pocatello, the city I grew up in that I didn't always appreciate, but have finally begun to understand that the inspiration was all around me and the potential is here. I was really reminded of why I love history and this community.

To all the people who indirectly helped me, both knowingly and unknowingly, over the years, that sense of adventure was harnessed during the research for this book.

Thanks, Caleb, for letting me borrow your drone.

It was really amazing seeing how much love there is for Pocatello and all the people in Facebook groups who were happy and excited to share pictures, facts, and stories. It really made it difficult to complete this book because there is just so much to know and share. This doesn't even cover a fraction of what I would like it to, but it is a start.

Unless otherwise noted, all images are from the author's personal collection.

Introduction

Pocatello, nicknamed the "Gate City" because of its importance for rail and wagon transportation to the Pacific Northwest, has had its fair share of ups and downs, like any other city. Named after a Shoshone chief, the town was established not far from the abandoned Fort Hall, familiar to anyone who played the game *The Oregon Trail*. Nestled in the Portneuf Valley, the site was chosen by the railroad as a hub, in part because of its location on the California and Oregon Trails.

With both major trails passing through the area, the valley saw fairly high traffic. Gold, and eventually other minerals of importance, were found in the area and helped to bring even more people. After the gold craze died down, the people who remained turned to agriculture.

Though it started with some controversy due to the reservation being nearby, Chief Pocatello gave land for the railroad to start building throughout the valley. A small plot of the current downtown was given to the railroad. For the city to grow and expand, it would take up more reservation land twice over the years. Currently, the reservation is around Pocatello to the west and north, just outside town limits. The town was able to grow more as land from the reservation was handed over.

The Utah and Northern Line was the first railroad established in the area, in 1878. In 1881, the Oregon Short Line (OSL), a subsidiary of Union Pacific (UP), decided to start expanding across Idaho and through Pocatello. The growth of the steam engine contributed to the growth of Union Pacific and ultimately led to the growth of Pocatello. Pocatello had strong, consistent growth from the late 19th century into the early 20th century before plateauing. At its height in the 1950s, city officials even believed that Pocatello could become as large as Denver. But even with the prosperity of the postwar period, Pocatello would not quite reach that level of growth.

Pocatello was once known as a rough railroad town with gambling and prostitution. Eventually, more cultural activities sprouted up around town, including schools, theaters, and even a county courthouse. At one point, the largest rail center west of the Mississippi was here as well, but it was not to last.

Pocatello became an industrial and transportation center; because those would not last forever, some began to push for the establishment of an educational institution. Education grew to be of importance for the area. Idaho State University stepped up to help and eventually became the top employer in the area.

Extensive deposits of phosphate shale ore eventually brought J.R. Simplot and the FMC corporation to the area. This led to continued growth for Pocatello's industrial economy. Both became major employers, especially Simplot, a large employer in the state of Idaho. FMC has since closed, but Simplot is still a fairly major employer in the area. The city has since diversified into insurance and education.

Growing up, I had the normal teenage angst about my hometown. I could not wait to leave. After high school graduation and being gone for a few years, I was able to more wholly appreciate and be thankful for growing up in the Portneuf Valley. Pocatello has such a feeling of raw potential, you cannot help but feel motivated when visiting. Though Pocatello is not experiencing the same growth it once did, it is home to a strong and caring community—one that looks out for each other and thinks about how they can always be working to create a better home.

The idea for this book came after about 20 years of my Nana and Papa collecting Pocatello postcards from eBay. I remember when I would go over to stay with them and was very excited to see what new postcards had arrived since the last time I saw their collection. It was interesting learning so much history of the area piece by piece and picture by picture.

CHAPTER 1

BUILDING A CITY

THE RAILROAD COMES THROUGH

The Oregon Short Line freight depot at Pocatello is pictured in 1885. The depot was built between the tracks and had the Pacific Hotel just to the right. The tracks have three rails, which accommodated both narrow- and standard-gauge trains. Crossing the tracks was very dangerous, as people had to jump out of the way of trains. Eventually, a viaduct was built over the tracks, demolishing the depot and hotel.

The roundhouse was built in 1891, and in 1902, it was expanded. This was the beginning of what would become the largest Union Pacific hub west of Omaha. Unfortunately, operations in Pocatello have dwindled. Eventually, due to the lack of use of diesel engines and much less traffic, Union Pacific razed the roundhouse. Some evidence of it is still visible, but most of the structures of this important railroad hub are gone.

This shot from 1922 shows the Oregon Short Line Pocatello depot, built in 1915. Surprisingly, it took much longer than other cities for Pocatello to receive a proper stone depot building. More evidence of the important role Pocatello played for the railroad can be seen by all the rail cars going through. Today, a lot fewer rail cars move through Pocatello, and the tracks are largely empty. Unfortunately, passenger traffic through Pocatello has long since been discontinued.

As Pocatello was a thriving railroad town thanks to the Oregon Short Line, the population needed a respectable terminal for passenger travel. Built in 1915, the Union Depot now hosts Union Pacific offices. Pictured above is the OSL depot looking south across Pocatello Park in 1925. Today, the depot sees a lot less traffic, and is host to only offices for employees of Union Pacific.

As the railroad brought many goods and people through Pocatello, many cabs were needed to get people to and from the depot and around town. A Greyhound bus station was built in 1946 to help connect people to the trains, which can be seen at left above. Due to low ridership, Pocatello no longer has passenger rail service, and the Greyhound station has been sitting empty for a number of years. The photograph below is from 1926.

Looking down the rails behind the depot below, passenger cars have recently arrived and are about to go on their way. There have been a few attempts at returning passenger rail service, but none have been successful. Quite a few wagons can be seen lined up on the left, ready to haul luggage to and from the trains. The back of the depot had a storage room for passenger luggage. After the end of passenger service, it was demolished.

Rail cars would be left off to roll down a hill known as "the hump." The new yard seen here was opened in 1947. The towers on the left were for workers to oversee the yard. As part of the decommissioning of the Pocatello rail yards in the 1990s, the yard was reduced from 40 to 28 tracks. Eventually, in 2011, the rest of the yard and tracks were removed, and all that remains are a few power line towers in the distance.

The Union Pacific smokestack is seen here in 1957 from the Gould Street overpass. Once part of a power plant for a large and fully operational rail yard, this smokestack is one of the few remains of what used to be. As many Union Pacific buildings were starting to disappear, the president of UP at the time decided to save the power plant chimney from demolition and have it painted with "Union Pacific" so that it could be seen from the interstate.

CHAPTER 2

Educating a Community

Idaho State University

Seen here in 1915, the Academy of Idaho started in 1901 and is today known as Idaho State University (ISU). Theodore F. Turner, an Idaho state senator and mayor of Pocatello, worked hard to establish the university in Pocatello. The Academy of Idaho grew through a few names and eventually became Idaho State University in 1963. ISU is now a main job supplier, an economic powerhouse, and a growth supporter for Pocatello.

Turner Hall was built in 1903 and dedicated to Theodore Turner. Built as a girl's dormitory, it could house 74 women. Due to financial constraints during the Great Depression, Turner Hall was closed. Eventually, it deteriorated so badly that it was torn down in 1966, with a new dorm sporting the same name opening in 1967 on upper campus. Currently, the area is the College of Business Administration building, consisting mainly of classrooms and computer labs.

Idaho Technical School is pictured here in 1909. Currently the quad, this picture shows what was basically the entire school at the time from Red Hill. After being founded in 1901, Idaho Technical School went through a fairly quick growth spurt. Turner Hall, Swanson Hall, and Faris Hall are the three larger buildings from left to right. Unfortunately, most of the buildings seen here have all been razed. The center of the campus has shifted a bit south. Pocatello is visible in the distance.

Frazier Hall was built in 1924 as Idaho Technical Institute was really starting to expand, and was used for numerous theater productions in the growing school. Its stage was used for theater programs until the Stephens Performing Arts Center was opened in 2004. Currently, Frazier Hall, now called the Bilyeu Theatre, is used for classes, as is the stage. Red Hill can be seen in the background behind the chimney.

Here is the institute's first men's dorm in 1915. Faris Hall opened with 25 rooms in 1906. This was the second structure built on campus. As the university began to grow and expand, a new dorm to replace Faris Hall was built on upper campus. Razed in 1959, the Physical Science building was built to complement the quad, which features buildings holding classrooms and labs.

This postcard from 1920 is incorrectly labeled Residence Hall, which was farther south down the street and is now a parking lot. This is actually Colonial Hall, which was built in 1925 as a dorm. The new dorm was needed as the institute was rapidly growing and expanding. Residence Hall was very similar but without the entryway columns. Colonial Hall is currently an administrative office building for the university.

The College of Pharmacy started in 1920 with three students. After moving multiple times between various buildings, the college finally received its own building, which opened in 1943. With a new pharmacy building on the quad, this was the beginning of a strong medical school at the University of Idaho: Southern Branch. The pharmacy program started at ISU and helped contribute to the university being well known today in the medical field.

The original student union building was erected in 1939 for the University of Idaho: Southern Branch, as the school was going through a period of rapid growth. It is one of the oldest buildings on campus, as most of the original buildings have been razed. To accommodate even more growth and modernization, a new student union building was constructed in 1958 just south down the quad. In 1961, this structure became an administrative building for the college.

The first building wholly dedicated to a full library, seen here in 1958, was built in 1954 after the library had been in two other buildings. Eventually, more space was needed. Another building was erected, and the library moved again, in 1977. Around this time, a connecter to the new student union building was also constructed, connecting the two. Now the building is home to the Idaho Museum of Natural History.

The quad is pictured here in its almost-completed state and before demolitions began. On the left is Swanson Hall, the first building completed when the Academy of Idaho was started. It was razed in 1973. The arch of Swanson Hall was preserved, and students walk through it to begin their time at ISU. On the right is the original student union building, currently an administration building.

As the school began to grow, more buildings were being erected farther east and up the hill. Eventually, more men's dorms were constructed in that direction as well. Here, in 1963, are Nichols Hall on the left and Owen-Redfield Hall on the right, two of the first dorms to be built on upper campus. Currently, these dorms are coed and targeted at freshmen looking for a smaller community.

Davis Field was built in 1936 and originally called the Spud Bowl. It was used for all outdoor sports and is now used for track and field and the women's soccer team. This view is from the famous Red Hill in the 1960s. From here, one can see west to the foothills.

The current student union building (or SUB), named after Earl Pond, opened in 1958 and serves as the social, cultural, and recreational center of campus for students, faculty, alumni, and guests of the university. Currently, the SUB is a popular place for students and high school students to go bowling and play ping pong and billiards. A movie theater was added, and a child development center was built with a connecter. Red Hill can be seen in the background with an "I," which was recently updated and is now orange.

The second Reed Gym was built in 1951 to replace the original building on lower campus near the quad. This was the last building on campus to be designed by Frank Paradice. It has had several additions over the years, but the style and character have been preserved. Besides being a recreational building for students, Reed Gym is also the host of the basketball, volleyball, and tennis teams.

The quad as seen here is similar to how it looks today. Swanson and Turner Halls are pictured before they were razed, and Pocatello can be seen in the distance. The building on the left is the original library, now the Natural History Museum, and next to that is the pharmacy building. To the right, from the bottom, are Graveley Hall, dorms, and the first student union, which is now an administrative building.

This is a view of upper campus from Red Hill. From left to right in the background are the College of Technology, an old airplane hangar, Holt Arena, the new Turner Hall, and another dorm building. In the center is Cadet Field and Reed Gym. From left to right in the foreground are Nichols, Owen-Redfield, and Dyer Halls. This is a great view of the upper campus. Red Hill has long been a favorite spot for pictures of Idaho State University, Pocatello, and Portneuf Valley.

CHAPTER 3

VACATIONS

MOTELS

05. VIEW FROM THE VIADUCT BY NIGHT, POCATELLO, IDAHO.

This "view" from 1912 is what was imagined Pocatello would look like headed west down the viaduct. The Bannock Hotel, built in 1921 to replace the old Bannock Hotel, which went by many different names, was once the tallest building in Pocatello at seven stories. Only the center tower of the planned three was ever built. The hotel was known for luxury and had all of the modern conveniences that technology could supply. It was even expanded to have a drive-in motel in the back. Due to hard financial times, the hotel was demolished in 1982.

Once the tallest building in Pocatello, the Bannock Hotel, pictured here in 1931, is now Simplot Square. Eventually, the J.R. Simplot Company came to own the building and had it demolished in 1982. The land was then donated to the city, and the current Simplot Square was completed in 1989. This is one of the most changed blocks in Old Town. With the razing of the Bannock Hotel, about four buildings were also razed.

The Idaho Motor Court, seen here in the 1930s, is now a Taco Bell and Jackson's convenience store and Shell gas station The remnants behind the Taco Bell are now apartments. The plot of land between Fourth and Fifth Avenues near Idaho State University hosted many motels, as it is where the highway passed through. With the rise of the automobile, people were driving and staying in motels along the highway more instead of downtown near the train depot.

Hotel Yellowstone was built in 1915. It was once a grand hotel just outside the depot welcoming train passengers. It is seen in the 1950s, with shops and a cafe downstairs. Interestingly, the main entrance can be seen here with an awning and sign; today, the main entrance is on Main Street, to the left of the building. Currently, a restaurant, whiskey bar, and brewery operate on the main floor.

The Lazy Dutchmen Motel, seen here in the 1950s, was originally a hotel for travelers on the west side of Pocatello, usually traveling along US Highway 30 West. It was built out on the west end by itself and was a popular place for many people to live when they first moved to Pocatello. The building has since been converted to apartments and is now considered the outskirts of town.

The Sunset Motel, seen here in 1958, was built in a strip of motels between Fourth and Fifth Avenues for travelers driving the highway through Pocatello. Some remain, but most that are still standing have been converted to apartments, with a few even owned by the university. The Sunset has been demolished and rebuilt as another hotel. This was a common area to stay, as it was out of downtown but right on the highway. Plus, its close proximity to Idaho State University makes it convenient.

The Imperial 400 Motel was another motel built outside of downtown on the highway and close to the Idaho State University campus. In the 1960s, Imperial claimed to be "America's fastest-growing partnership chain." This strip of motels was built as the automobile became popular and people started bypassing the downtown area. This motel was demolished in the early 2010s for expansion of the McDonald's that shared the block.

The Pinecrest motel, seen here in 1961, was part of a trend of motels being built north along the highway even farther away from downtown. At first, this strip of the highway was pretty empty, as most traffic went through downtown. Eventually, Yellowstone Highway became home to multiple motels and eventually replaced downtown as the main stretch of commerce. The Pinecrest has been replaced by a couple of restaurants.

Pictured is the Bannock Motor Inn, with the Hotel Bannock in the background, in 1968. The Bannock Motor Inn was an extension of the hotel targeted at motorists driving through. It was in the heart of the city and boasted many amenities, such as a heated pool, color TV, courtesy car, lounge, coffee shop, dining room, convention space and meeting room with a capacity of 750, a gift shop, and a barbershop. The Bannock Motor Inn was built to compete with other motor inns on Yellowstone in an attempt to bring traffic back to downtown.

The Pocatello Travel Lodge, seen here in 1963, offered amenities that the hotels downtown could not compete with. It featured ample parking and even a pool. The shift away from traveling through on the train and staying downtown had begun. The lodge was one of the first to remain near downtown instead of out on the highway, but also offered easy highway access. Currently, the lodge is now apartments, and unfortunately, the pool has been permanently drained and filled.

Seen here in 1963, the Howell Motel had joined a growing list of motels built on the highway to bypass downtown altogether. When the Howell was originally built, Alameda, the cross street just to the right, was still a dirt road and out of city limits. It would take a few years for this area of Yellowstone to build up, but it eventually became the main commercial strip in Pocatello.

The Idaho Motel was located at 1159 South Fifth Avenue in 1962. At its height, it had 32 insulated, air-conditioned, carpeted units with TV and phones in every room and even some units with kitchens. An advertisement claimed that it was "Next to Idaho State College on Highways 91, 191, 30N. Accepting Diners' Club, American Express and Carte Blanche credit cards." Today, the site is home to a Taco Bell.

The Thunderbird Motel was another auto inn built for travelers driving through Pocatello and looking to stay near Idaho State University. There have been a few changes, but for the most part, the Thunderbird has stayed the same. The pool has been drained and the sign moved, but it is one of the few in the area that is still operated as a motel and is locally owned.

Bidwell's Auto Court, one of the first auto courts in the area, is seen here in the 1940s. It was built next to the school to target travelers driving through on the highway and not looking to go downtown. Bidwell's was built along the highway near the university and on the east side of Pocatello. Most of the original auto court has been demolished, but there is a small portion left that, similar to many other old motels in the area, is now apartments.

CHAPTER 4

BLAST FROM THE PAST

OLD TOWN

As Pocatello was growing on both the west and east sides of the tracks, crossings were increasing, and unfortunately, so were casualties. To help solve this problem, a viaduct was built across the tracks on Center Street. Here is the viaduct in the 1920s after it was built in 1911. It helped keep Pocatello connected until the Center Street underpass replaced it in 1934. On the far left, the old depot can be seen, and next to it is the Pacific Hotel. Part of the Pacific Hotel was demolished to build this viaduct and the rest of the hotel was razed before the underpass was completed.

West Center Street is seen facing east in 1907. This was really the beginning of growth for the downtown area. At the end of the street is the old Pacific Hotel, which was partially demolished to build the Center Street viaduct before being completely razed so the viaduct could be replaced with the current underpass. The underpass can be seen below. Most of these buildings have since been demolished.

The Railroad Young Men's Christian Association (RRYMCA) was built in the budding downtown in 1907 to provide a recreation spot for the many railroad workers of the Oregon Short Line living and traveling through the area. Here is the building in the 1920s. It was demolished in 1986. An arch was built as a remembrance, with the initials RRYMCA. It serves as an entrance to the parking lot that is now there.

The Pocatello library was originally built in 1907 with funding by Andrew Carnegie, who had helped fund many libraries around the world. The house to the left was donated and available for the librarian to live in. An addition and atrium were built in 1993 to expand usable space. For a few years, this was the main library, but it is now the only one in town. Currently, the original building is used as offices for library staff.

This view of Main Street in 1909 looks north. The Paris can be seen on the right at Center Street. The building on the right with the awnings is the Princess Theater, which Judy Garland sang about in *A Star is Born*, released in 1954. After a fire at the theater, the building had an expansion added to the top and became the Whitman Hotel. After a renovation in the early 2010s, it reopened as the Whitman Apartments.

This view looks west up Center Street to the west bench in 1910. At the time, this was the view coming down the viaduct; now, it is the view coming out of the underpass. Many of the stone and brick buildings look much as they do today. All of the wooden buildings, though, have since been replaced. Idaho Furniture Co., the stone building at right, was the Paris department store.

The library can be seen here in 1916 on the left. This photograph was taken from the rooftop of the first Bannock Hotel before it was added to and later razed. The tall apartment building on the right and the library are the only two buildings still standing. The building on the bottom and church on the left are now just parking lots. Most of the houses have also been replaced.

The downtown Episcopal church seen here in 1912 was built in 1898. It is across the street from Pocatello High School. The original church was moved to the lot next to this new building in 1900. The small building to the right of the church has since been demolished and is now a small park with a basketball court. In the mid-1930s, the present parish hall was built. On the far right is the tower of the former downtown fire station.

The telephone building is seen here in 1917. The building was razed and rebuilt on the back of the block. Now, a drive-through coffee shop and a parking lot have replaced the original building. The current telephone building can be seen in the background. The houses to the left and behind the old telephone building have all been demolished. Three of the four buildings that were on this corner have been demolished.

Arthur Street is seen here looking north in 1919, with an "X" to mark the Bannock Hotel. The only building still standing today on the right has a "C" painted on its side. The Valentine Building on the left is still standing; it was initially built for First National Bank and is an office building now. The Kasiska Building across the street, past the bank, has since been razed.

Every rapidly growing city needs a post office and courthouse. Pictured here in 1916, shortly after completion, is a US post office and courthouse in the ever-expanding downtown. While not nearly as ornate as others around the country, it was still functional. The addition on the left and back was built in 1937. Today, the building is used as an office building for local companies, while the main floor that was the post office and then a bar/restaurant sits empty.

Built in 1914 and eventually demolished due to a fire in the 1990s, the Kasiska Building at 345 West Lewis Street is seen here in the 1920s. It was named for William F. Kasiska, an immigrant from East Prussia who became a well-known businessman in Pocatello. The building was erected by Frank Paradice, who also designed multiple buildings for Idaho State University. It housed not only his architectural offices, but also a drug company.

This view of East Center Street looks west in the 1920s. This side of the tracks did not build up as much as the downtown in the west. The east side mainly had Center Street as the main area and was originally connected by an overpass that would then be demolished for the current underpass. Of the buildings that are still standing, most have bars on the main level, while some have apartments upstairs or empty upper floors.

This view of Center Street looks west across the highway in 1935. Looking down the street, the Center Street viaduct is gone, as the current underpass replaced it in 1934. Just to the right out of the picture is where the Bannock County Courthouse was built. Center Street was a popular route for many years, connecting the west and east sides of the city. The service station on the left is now the parking lot for the Bannock County Juvenile Center.

The Center Street viaduct was built in 1911 and created a safe passage between east and west Pocatello. Before it was built, crossing the tracks was quite dangerous, as people had to constantly jump out of the way of many moving trains. This photograph from the 1930s was taken shortly before the viaduct was demolished to be replaced with the current underpass. This view is from the roof of the Central Building.

This view of Pocatello looks east from the west bench in the 1930s. The photographs are taken from a former popular lookout known as the "Stairway to Heaven." Originally, the stairs led to a dance hall and offered an amazing panoramic view of the Portneuf Valley, including Pocatello. Benton Street is on the left with an overpass over the tracks. Halliday Street, on the right, used to have an underpass under the tracks. The building in the middle was originally Emerson Elementary School and then a school run by Franciscan sisters, but is now empty.

Seen here is the Wholesale District, now the Warehouse District, on the east side of the tracks, in a view looking north along First Street in 1932. This area was known for warehouses with easy access to the railroad. The warehouse on the right had a clock installed and is currently the home of the Don Aslett Museum of Clean. As the railroads left, so did much of the need for this district. Currently in the area are some offices, storage, a brewery, and a gymnastics gym.

This is a view looking west toward the corner of Center and Main Streets after coming out of the newly built underpass. At the time, Center Street was two-way, but it is now one-way headed west. Main Street was also a two-way street but is now one-way headed north. Like many cities around the country, this was a time of economic growth for Pocatello. As seen here in 1943, this was an area that saw a lot of traffic.

This night view of Center Street looks west. Both Center and Main Streets were known for having many fluorescent lights. Center Street was a two-way street but is now one-way heading west. After many businesses left downtown for the nearby Yellowstone Highway, many lights started to disappear. In 2012, a local organization, Relight the Night, started to work to get the lights refurbished, reinstalled, and relit, with 17 completed so far.

Even with the nearby Yellowstone Highway beginning to take away a lot of downtown business, this corner of Center and Main Streets was still seeing quite a bit of activity in the 1950s. This was just about the beginning of shops and signs coming down. This view looks west just after emerging from the Center Street underpass. Main Street has already transitioned to one-way, but Center Street is still two-way.

Main Street is seen here in the 1950s looking south shortly after becoming a one-way street. There are still many signs of activity in the downtown area, as shops and restaurants were just starting to open up on Yellowstone Highway. Many buildings still had big signs to help customers find businesses. Some of the buildings have been altered a bit for current uses, but for the most part, they are still the same.

This photograph of Main Street, facing north in the 1950s, is just down the block and looks in the opposite direction of the views on the previous page. The Paris, on the right, is in the second oldest building in the city. The Paris was a shopping staple for many years before closing and remaining empty for a spell. Now, it is a record/antique store with a café. Peterson's Furniture was also a staple for many years before turning into a sports shop, but it is now empty.

This view of Main Street looks north in the early 1950s. The Whitman Hotel is an interesting building, as it used to be the Princess Theatre. In popular culture, it became famous for a Judy Garland song in the movie *A Star is Born*. In the song "Born in a Trunk," Garland says she was born in a trunk in the Princess Theatre in Pocatello. After a fire, the building then became the Whitman Hotel. After renovation, it reopened as apartments.

This view of West Center Street looks east in 1961. The Bannock Hotel, on the right, was still the tallest building in town. The Bannock was demolished in 1982 and is now Simplot Square. The Carnes Music building on the left was also razed, and a bank was built in its place. This area of town does not see the amount of traffic that it once did. The Center Street underpass can almost be seen at the end of the street.

This 1963 photograph of Center Street looks east. The number of signs indicate the level of activity of the city. Similar to Main Street and East Center Street, West Center Street was a very busy corridor. Besides all of the signs being gone, the building to the immediate left was demolished and replaced with a large bank building. This is a prime example of how much the character of downtown has changed.

The Chief Theater, at 217 North Main Street, is pictured in 1980. The Chief, with its dazzling glazed terra-cotta front and neon marquee, opened in 1938 with a Wallace Beery movie and continued showing movies into the 1980s. During a remodel in 1993 to become a community arts center, it caught fire and burned down. Currently, the space is a parking lot, with the floor mosaic and a sign as part of Relight the Night.

CHAPTER 5

IMAGES FOR THE WORLD

POSTCARDS

This image was captured from the base of the viaduct, looking west, in 1919, depicting the hustle and bustle that used to be Pocatello. The Center Street viaduct was an important way for people to cross the train tracks and connect east and west Pocatello; thus, it is a very busy and important corridor. The Monarch Hotel can be seen on the right, with part of a pointing hand on the wall. It lost its roof in a 2014 fire.

This view looks east down Center Street and the train tracks around 1900. The old Pacific Hotel can be seen, which had its south (right) end removed for the construction of the Center Street viaduct that opened in 1911. The rest of the Pacific Hotel was removed so the railroad would have more space. In 1934, the viaduct was razed for the underpass that is in place today.

By the early 1900s, Pocatello was starting to grow and had the downtown to prove it. On Main Street, in this view looking north, a few staples of the budding town can be seen. Even parts of today's downtown can be seen, such as the Paris at right, built in 1892, and Petersen Furniture, which until recently was Scott's Ski and Sports but is now empty. These city streets were very wide, especially since motor vehicles were rare at the time.

The original Bannock County Courthouse, built in 1902, is seen here shortly after completion. It was razed so that the current one could be built in 1954. When the original courthouse was built, the block had many trees, creating a park that took up the entire block. The county courthouse was built on the east side of the tracks, which at the time was mostly empty fields. Center Street, in front of the courthouse, was built up over the years.

The Auditorium Theatre was built in 1890 and suffered fires in 1892 and 1899. Harry Houdini performed here in 1924. After a third fire in 1939, the third floor was removed, and it became a store. It was most recently a furniture store but now sits empty. A "fire phantom" has been blamed as the cause of the multiple fires on this lot and in a few other theaters around Pocatello.

Pocatello High School was originally built in 1892. The building was a meeting place for the city and even hosted two presidential speeches: Pres. Theodore Roosevelt in 1902 and Pres. William Howard Taft in 1908. A fire in 1914 burned most of the structure, but it was rebuilt. An expansion consisting of a new gym, cafeteria, and auditorium came in 1938 thanks to a Public Works Administration project. Another gym came in 2004, and currently another expansion to connect all the buildings across Lander Street is in progress.

The original Pocatello Masonic Temple, opened in 1903, is seen here in 1909. After a fire in 1922, the building reopened and was then reconfigured in 1927. The first floor was a furniture company, the second was a hotel, and the third floor hosted the Masons. The building is currently owned by Pocatello Electric, in operation for over a century. Across the street was one of Idaho's first chapters of the International Order of Odd Fellows.

The Pioneer Building was erected in 1892 as Pocatello was growing to become the primary trade center of southwestern Idaho. In 1909, it was the First National Bank, but it is now home to a post office on the ground floor and empty above. When the bank first opened, it was given five years of free rent. In April 1915, the bank merged with Famers and Traders Bank and moved to the Valentine Building on Arthur Street.

The Seavers Building was constructed in 1900. This postcard image looks west down Center Street in 1910. The building is best remembered for the Temple Pharmacy that occupied it for many years. At one point, this building was described as "intrusive" and had even been targeted for demolition. Because of a restoration/renovation project, it was saved. After sitting empty for a number of years, the United Way of Southeastern Idaho moved in.

The new Center Street viaduct is seen in 1911 looking east toward the east bench. Having a safe way to cross the tracks was welcomed by people in town, as it was dangerous dodging trains. The Auditorium Theatre can be seen just above the bridge. The remaining part of the Pacific Hotel that was partially demolished for the viaduct is just the left of it. The house to the right of the viaduct is now a park.

The Center Street viaduct is seen here in 1920 looking west toward the west bench. Not only did the viaduct make it safe for pedestrians to cross the tracks, but now cars could cross without having to go down and around. In 1934, the viaduct was replaced with an underpass. Today, the underpass is a crucial connection between east and west Pocatello (downtown).

East Center Street has changed more than its west counterpart through the years due to buildings being razed or altered. This view in 1916 from the viaduct looks east. The Auditorium Theater is the tallest building on the right. The steeple behind the theater is the Pocatello House Hotel. Center Street was usually abuzz with activity during this time, as the city was growing and Center Street provided easy access, connecting west and east Pocatello.

This view of Center Street looks east from the foothills of the west bench in 1913. All of these houses have since been replaced by other houses or other buildings. The tallish building on the left is the original Pocatello High School. Up Center Street is the former viaduct that was still fairly new at the time. It is also very noticeable how much Pocatello has expanded to the east and up the east bench.

This image looks west down Center Street from the bottom of the viaduct in the 1920s. Besides the buildings on the front left of the postcard, most of the buildings are still standing today. The Monarch Hotel with "Hayes" painted on the side caught fire in 2014, and part of the wall that fell can be seen. There are efforts to restore the building and reopen it as a hotel.

From the roof of the Carlson Building, this view looks east up Center Street in 1921. The newly built depot building is on the upper right of the postcard, with trains behind. The Valentine Building in the bottom right is still standing, but the connected brick building was not as lucky. As Center Street was important and busy, many signs lined the street.

This view looks north on Main Street in 1928. Fargo's was a popular department store built in 1916. While the main floor was a department store, the upstairs were apartments. The building has since been converted to a shopping mall with offices, shops, restaurants, and a salon. Unfortunately, the buildings on the left side of the block were not able to survive. That block is now a bank office and parking lot.

This view of Center Street looks east from Arthur Street in the early 1930s. Since there is no viaduct, the image dates to the construction of the underpass or shortly after it opened. The Valentine Building is the white building on the right. By this time, First National Bank was operating out of it. The drugstore that was connected was unfortunately demolished and a new, smaller drugstore is now in its place. The entire left side of the block was demolished and is now a bank.

This 1930s image looks north on Main Street. This is almost the same shot as seen on page 90. Pocatello was going through a period of rapid growth, and in the short span of a decade, there were already noticeable changes. Fargo's, a staple, is still there, but one can see how much the roads have been upgraded, as well as the stoplights. The cross street is Lewis Street, and the first block on the left has unfortunately been razed.

This view of Main Street looks south in 1936. The stone building on the left was erected in about 1894 and operated primarily as a meat butcher. Through the early 20th century, it changed businesses a few times. Since 1946, though, it was the Oasis Bar. Upstairs was originally the RRYMCA before it got its own building. Across the street above it is the original Pocatello Masonic Temple. Across from that to the right is the International Order of Odd Fellows. The J.C. Penney is now just a parking lot.

This 1940s photograph of Arthur Street looks north. The post office and courthouse are on the right with their fairly new addition. The building behind that has been demolished. The extravagant building on the left is the Bannock Hotel, with the only completed tower of the planned three. The one-story building to the left of it and the two buildings on the right, including the tall one, were all demolished to create Simplot Square.

This view of Center Street looks east toward the underpass in the 1940s. The clock on the left was part of Molinelli's Jewelers. Since that building has been demolished, Molinelli's and the clock were moved around the corner to Main Street. The rest of the buildings on the left side of the block still stand, but look different. The Cook Drug Co., advertising Kodaks, is now Maag pharmacy, a staple of Pocatello. The white Valentine Building is to the right.

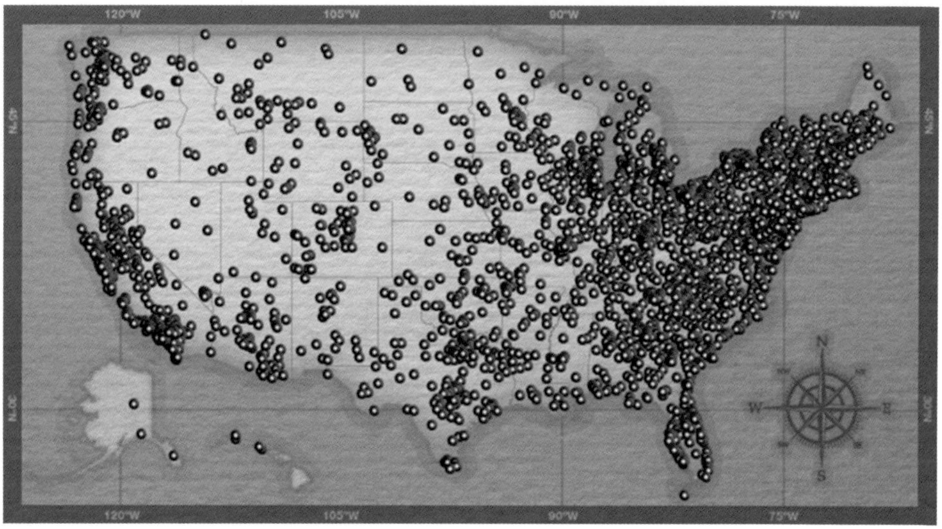